Battle Cancer

Journey to a New Life

Rosalind's Victory Journal

Written by

Rosalind B. Pettiford, Survivor

Designed and Edited by
Celeste Morris

Graphics by
Djenee Dunn, Tamu Creative

Amazing Journey Publishing

Battle Cancer: Journey to a New Life

First Printing: 2020

ISBN: 978-1-7923-1149-9

Amazing Journey Publishing

Brooklyn, NY

www.amazingjourney.com

Dedicated to

My father James W. Bostic Sr. who showed me how to battle cancer with grace and faith; my grandmother, Irene Munroe, who never said the word cancer while she battled for years; my Sister Irene Perry who fought a tough cancer battle and left us in August 2010.

Acknowledgements

First and foremost I would like to thank GOD, all that I do is because of GOD. No one wants Cancer in order to find purpose. A broken woman asked GOD to use her if she survived Cancer and He is doing just that.

I would like to thank my children, the three of my womb -- Craig, Tyson and Tierra and the two of my heart Tanya and Belvia. You have made this Journey even better because of your love, concern and growth with me along the way.

No one writes a book without help. Denise Hinton (an Author with three books of poems to her name) has been my biggest cheerleader with this Journal for the last six years. Even when I doubted myself, she pushed and encouraged me.

Sometimes we don't think we are good enough or smart enough and the right Angels come our way. In November of 2018 I was having a shower meeting with GOD and informed him that I badly needed an Editor. I wasn't happy with recommendations that I had received. 24 hours later Celeste Morris, a friend and former employer that I hadn't seen in over twenty years was volunteering at my church. During our conversation, I told her about my journal and needing an editor. She immediately said she would do it!

My computer Angel is Ordonna Hinton Sargeant. No one can take me out of computer purgatory like she can.

Others in my village that I must thank: my cousin Jeanette Mann George, who believed in me when I didn't believe in me (she and Denise both told me that this Journal would help others); Rev. Dr. Christine Caton, for being a Mentor, Friend and personal library for all things Cancer; to Betty Jones for being such a support when I needed her the most (decades of friendship); to my Sisters in Christ at First Baptist Church of Crown Heights (too many to name) who always encourage me in so many ways. Thank you for your hugs. You know I love them. And to all my friends that stuck with me when the going got scary, I thank you.

A special salute to all the beautiful souls that I have met along this Journey that are no longer here and all the ones that are still in the battle.

My sincere and deepest gratitude to the Cancer Ministry of First Baptist Church of Crown Heights for allowing me to lead and live the dream of reaching back and helping others

I would like to thank every kind doctor, nurse or medical personnel that helped me along the way especially Dr. Pothuri, Dr. Freedman, Kathleen Lutz PA and the wonderful staff at New York University Cancer Center.

FINALLY: No one walks this path alone. Be kind we are all going home together one step at a time.

Introduction

Years ago the word Cancer meant a death sentence. Today the word cancer is everywhere - in conversations, news, movies, political campaigns, the internet, and social media. There isn't a major television show that does not address the issue of CANCER. If you have been in this battle, when you hear the word your dog ears go up. I wasn't new to the word cancer. I heard it first when I was 6 months old when my paternal grandmother died at home from ovarian cancer.

I have always kept a journal. In other days it was called a Diary. On November 2, 2009, I was diagnosed with uterine cancer. I started writing my journal on November 4th. I knew it would be therapeutic and it would be a way of keeping my thoughts of life, pain, anxiety, treatments, praise and gratitude along the journey. After being encouraged by friends and family that the written story of my journey might help others, I decided to share. My prayer is that someone will be encouraged by my story, that my Journey through this disease can show that the battle can be won and that this testimony can help others with their test. I decided to name my journal "Battle Cancer" because it is a fight! Those I have met through this Journey have countless stories of the battle they fought with hope, dignity, faith, family and encouragement.

This book is subtitled

A VICTORY JOURNAL

"You Came, We Fought, I Won"

You came: You knocked me to my feet and turned my life upside down, you brought your friend Fear along with you and though my children were grown you made me worry about them.

We fought: I had a complete hysterectomy, three rounds of chemotherapy, a lumpectomy, a spot on my lung, a thyroid biopsy, and more CAT scans that I can count.

I WON: The battle, found purpose, created a ministry, experienced enormous growth, and gained even more compassion and faith than I ever had before.

Welcome to MY Journal and My Journey

The Journey

Wednesday, November 4, 2009 8:00 AM

"...the battle is not yours it's the Lord's"! On Friday I survived a crane accident on the Brooklyn Queens Expressway. A flatbed truck had a crane tied down on it, that hit an overpass, broke free and then hit my car. Had I not seen it coming and drove fast the story end would be different. Less than 72 hours later I found out that I had another battle on my hands. Instead of battle crane, it's battle CANCER (Uterine).

One of my favorite shows on cable TV is Iron Chef America, where top chefs battle against each other. The chairman picks ingredients and the chefs battle to make different dishes to see who will win.

My life has been a few battles over the last 3 years, but my faith has pulled me through. Sunday the message in church dealt with fighting the devil. Three quotes that I wrote down that day: (1) the devil will get tired of me soon, (2) he has not broken me yet, (3) I already have the victory. Little did I know how important these 3 quotes would become.

So, battle cancer begins.

The top Chef (Jesus) and his busy opponent (the devil), along with the ingredient (cancer) have started the battle. I know by watching previous shows of my life who will win. My youngest daughter, Tierra, was with me when I got the news. She was my rock that day and I'm so proud of her. She is dealing with major stuff in her life and still she rises to help and comfort me. As I told my children and two close friends, my faith and theirs became stronger. Come on cancer we are going to kick your butt.

I have not told other family members yet. On November 3rd we went to a funeral for my sister Nanette's good friend and college buddy that battled stomach cancer. So, it is not the time yet.

The cancer for my battle is uterine stage 1. With a complete hysterectomy I will be cured. Dr. Friedman does not believe that it has spread. If the tests are right, I won't need chemotherapy. My mother's mother, my father's mother and my father have all lost battles with cancer. My sister beat breast cancer 5 years ago with no return.

I have taken a medical leave from my job (that I've had for only 18 months) to take tests and to live and laugh until the surgery. I want to change directions in my life and speak to women about cancer and healing. I want to spend more time with family and friends and write all the books I said I would. I want to create a line of inspirational t-shirts. I want to see my gifted grandson who is 6 years old, graduate from college and hold his children on my lap. I want to smell the breath of my friend Cheyenne's baby (due in May). I have always enjoyed life no matter what's going on and I still will.

P.S. I want to wear a beaded dress to my younger son's wedding.

Monday, November 9, 2009 6:54 PM

I have cancer but cancer does not have me. I told my sister Nanette last night; she did not take it well. She just lost a good friend to cancer. I told my mother this morning and she took it better than I thought she might. Told Matthew today over the phone, I could hear the shock in his voice. We are married, but separated, he lives in Trinidad.

Last night was the first night I woke up in the middle of the night with negative thoughts, I went back to sleep and didn't wake up until the alarm went off. A strange thing happened Wednesday night. I was sleeping in the chair and I heard a voice say out loud, they didn't get it all. I don't know if I was dreaming but it sure woke me up. I told the devil this is not going to control my mind. I plan to win this battle.

When I left the house today to take a walk, I told my mother not to worry, "I'm going to win this battle". I really feel positive but at times my mind runs wild. I'm only human and a little scared. Thursday and Friday, I'm in Atlantic City and I almost forget that I have cancer. I'm enjoying eating (far too much), talking with people and sleeping, watching the ocean, television, taking showers and best of all playing poker. After the whole trip I came out losing $15 including food and tips. Thank GOD for that too.

Everyone says that they are praying for me and I believe them too.

I found out that my insurance only pays 75% of the bill but that's not going to be a problem because I'm putting that in GOD's hands.

Tuesday, November 10, 2009 11:56 PM

SCARED. My appointment with the Surgeon is in the morning at 9:45. I keep forgetting that I have cancer but the calls from the doctor's office make me remember. My son, Craig, took the Mothers out for dinner tonight (his mother-in-law and me). It was really nice. Thank GOD for children. When I'm doing things like this I forget. My co-worker called tonight. She lost her mother to ovarian cancer when she was 12 years old. That cancer word is so nasty, but I plan to kick it in the butt. Stay tuned for the battle.

Monday, November 16, 2009 8:47 PM

Just spent the weekend with Betty - my spiritual rock. I love Betty for many reasons but the main one is that she does not judge, and she is so easy to spend time with. I drove myself to get a scan today, a little shaky on the highway but not too bad. Went into my mother's room this morning to see how she is dealing with this. Talked to her about my faith in GOD and being me through this battle and how different people react. I explained that sometimes I really don't remember that I'm battling cancer. My sister-in-law said that's because even the word scares you.

I love my children. Each of them is handling their reaction to my diagnosis differently! Craig is the big strong rock of a son who shows no emotion, but I feel his pain miles away. Tyson, who can talk to me about female medical problems, informed me that he broke down the first night. He and his friend Jimmy went on the internet to do research. His friend Mike's mom called to tell him that she is surviving stage 3. Tierra, who bears such pain about this and was with me in the doctor's office, is showing such a brave front for me. I know that she is hurting because she watched her friend Jessie's father fade away and pass this year from cancer. I still have friends to call and inform and ask them to pray with me and for me.

November 17, 2009 10:15 AM

Sitting and waiting for blood work and EKG for medical clearance for the surgery. I'm having pain in my pelvic area and wondering if this is one of the side effects of this cancer. It wants to show its face now more than ever. It's saying, "Remember me". Too bad! The victory is already won. Cancer is a battle that has to be won with the 3 "S's", Spirit, Support and a Smile. If your spirit is strong you will keep going. If your support is strong it will carry you. If your smile is strong it will attract the people you deal with and they will help you with a smile.

Monday, November 23, 2009 10:10 PM: Surgery Day

"Give GOD the Glory"

Monday, November 30, 2009

I can't believe it has been a whole week. What a week it has been! Came out of surgery. Craig and Georgia were there. Betty came by later that night. Dr. Hope (check out the name) and Dr. Pothuri came by with good news, they believe they got it all, no signs that it went anywhere else.

"The victory is mine said the Lord!"

The morning of the surgery the devil tried to get his last bid in. I was told because I did not bring a check for $1,602 the finance department would not release my records for the surgery. I moved from the desk, prayed and went back but my records were still locked. The lady at the desk was name Frances she was kind and said it happens all the time that someone forgets to tell you to bring a check for your share of the room. As I got up to leave and pray again, she opened her drawer and she showed me her bible opened. I sat back down and then I pictured the door opening behind her. I said, "Francis in about 5 to 10 minutes that door is going to open and the nurse is coming out to call my name and to get me". In 7 minutes the door opened, my records were unlocked and my name was called.

Dr. Pothuri's team is just like her...top notch, humble and very caring. Pauline (the nurse who gets A+ in customer service) was like having a daughter in the operating room. Robotic surgery was done, and I go back in two weeks for post operation appointment. No radiation or chemo planned. When God is for you what can man do. I have been blessed this week as much as I have been blessed my whole life. Sometimes it takes a stand in the valley to see the mountain top.

This week I have heard stories of cancer that have made me realize that I am on the right path with "battle cancer". Many stories of misdiagnosed people who waited too long and really have to battle advanced stages past one. We need to learn to speak up for ourselves or find people we trust to speak for us.

My son Tyson has had the same core of friends for the last 16 years. 3 of them now live in Atlanta and two of them came to see me in NY this week. Mike brought his mother Pat Henry (a stage 3 uterine cancer survivor) when he came. We are now new BFFs. The doctors told her that her fibroids would shrink but she felt something was wrong. After researching and fighting for herself she found out that she had stage 3. Soon after surgery she had chemo. Today is one of her follow up visits. I pray for her healing as I pray for mine.

I met a woman named Patty through this journey, one of my new angels. What can I say about Patty? She is definitely a person to have on your team. She is special and no matter how long I live, I'll remember her and the personal care. She called and worked my case with the VA hospital like I was the only case she had for the last two weeks. I really love Patty. There are truly angels among us.

GOD has truly set me up with warriors on this battlefield.

My girlfriend Chris, who lives in Florida, was awakened at 4:00 am on Nov 23rd, (the day of my surgery). She pictured me going into surgery and prayed. I told her that I knew this had to be true. I never knew such peace going into surgery as I did that morning.

GOD bless and thanks to all the people who carried me up to the altars on Sunday Nov. 22, 2009. Barbara Johnson, Georgia Pullen, Betty Jones, Denise and Ordonna Hinton, Pearl Bostic, Nanette Egerton, Rose Gietchier, Rose McCleary, Gerald from the poker room in Atlantic City, Mike the poker player who told me his wife lit a candle for me, my brother Tommy and his wife Yolanda, and to all the others GOD put in my path. From the smiling faces of Dr. Friedman and his wonderful nurses, Carmen, Theresa and Josefee, to the tears of friends and family that went into battle with me, to the co-workers who called and prayed. Thanks, Natalie, for the voice message I heard the morning I was leaving for the hospital. Yvonne and Wendy Lou Leslie a mother and daughter team who have been my friends for more than 20 years. Thanks to the two of you for the flowers, tear soup and your love that have never failed me. Thanks Tyrone Pettiford. I saw the pain in your eyes when I told you I just battled cancer. Thanks Ms. Donna for sending your cell phone, your food and your strong shoulder for Tierra to lean on. Thanks, James, for looking in on me and helping me upstairs and for your smiles. Thanks, my loving daughters Tanya and Beliva for your prayers, love, food, laptop and smiles. Thanks, big Belvia for your words and thanks for telling me things while I was alive to hear them. Thanks, Matthew, for making me go to the Doctor's office when I was bleeding. Thank God for every Thanksgiving plate that was sent along with pies and sweets. Thanks, Lionel, for cheesecake and candles. Thanks Tierra and Castel for giving up your bedroom, taking great care of me, helping me put on my socks and pulling me up to stand. Thanks, Gietschier children for my strength bracelet that was the only thing I wore into surgery. Thanks, Arianna, for your version of GOD has smiled on me. (She's 21 months old.)

If GOD never does anything else, he has done enough already. It's my turn to live in purpose, the reason I am alive. You are right Arianna. GOD has smiled on me. Thanks, Craig, for spending 16 hours in the hospital while answering questions from everyone and dealing with your own emotions. Thanks, Nanette. Your recent battle with your friend is still in your heart (I understand). Thanks, Rose, for calling without knowing what to say but ending up asking to be invited to the victory party. Thanks, Keiko for telling me how brave I am and saying you wish you were brave. You are.

Thanks First Baptist Church of Crown Heights for being the place that put the spotlight on my prayers every time I walk into your doors. The praise in this church tells me that I have found home. Thanks to Betty for inviting me to this. The Gospel choir is about to get a new singer!

Thursday, December 10, 2009 1:35 PM

Yesterday was my post-surgery appointment. Tierra took me -- Looks like she's in charge of taking me to my appointments. Good news. Thank GOD, all the tissues tested show no signs of it going anywhere else. I'm healing well. I have a bad cold, so they checked me for pneumonia, all clear. I had uterine cancer which can be very aggressive and can come back in different parts of the body 35% of the time. So I will be the 65% that it won't return to (GOD's battle). I was feeling a little low about having to take a couple of rounds of chemo. People say that it can be worse than cancer. I go back to NYU next Wednesday 12/16. Dr. Pothuri and Nurse Kathleen will tell me which route they want to take, and we will discuss treatment. Betty said that she will take time off her job so that she can go with me to most of my visits. Here I go again being blessed again with support. Thank you, GOD.

On my way to the elevator feeling sorry for myself about chemo and learning that this cancer tries to come back. GOD put Elizabeth in my path. Elizabeth heard me discussing losing my hair, she said she's about to lose her hair again and not very happy about it. She's all of 5ft tall thick blond hair. She told me this would be her tenth round of chemo in 4 years. It started with breast cancer, now it's back in the bones and the liver. We hugged and I told her that I would pray for her. I told her to stay strong that she is a survivor. She told me she has to keep trying because she's addicted to this thing called life. My sister Irene said that we hold on to this thing called life because that's all we know. Irene is a 7-year breast cancer survivor. She told me to dress real nice when I go for treatment to cheer myself up.

I have asked Yvonne to go wig shopping with me. If it wasn't winter, I might go for the bald look. (Smile).

Spoke to Shantel, my co-worker, whose mother and grandmother have been through chemo. She said she knows the deal, but she said she knows that I'm strong.

Cheyenne called this week to confirm the baby is a girl - little Rosalind. Spoke to Pat Henry and she promised to stay in touch.

Thomasina a friend and cancer survivor spoke about this battle. She had breast cancer and her last round of chemo was 14 months ago, still clean thank GOD.

Tuesday, December 15, 2009 10:15 AM

GOD keeps blessing me with angels on earth. Nurse Wiggins came across my path on December 9 in the form of interviewing me for access-a-ride. This angel took at least 30 minutes out of her day to talk about cancer with me. She told me about wellness, taking care of myself and being a diva for the next 2 months. Question and answer period with her was like one-on-one at a health conference with only two people attending. I needed her in my life and GOD placed her there.

Today I'm in the doctor's office to find out about the plan for chemo and beyond. I'm writing in my journal while waiting for the doctor to come in. My dreams are starting again, the ones that I can see things that are about to happen. Last Thursday the 8th, I dreamt that Tierra's building manager asked Tierra for the apartment and she told him she was going to get a check on December 11th and he told her he could not wait. When I told Tierra the dream, she said, "Mom that's not possible because I am fighting with my employer about unemployment". Tierra called the next day to tell me it was good to have a praying Mother. Unemployment made a payment to her account. She won the case.

Dr. Pothuri told me that I will be taking 3 sessions of chemo - one every 21 days. I will lose my hair, and someone should come with me. She also told me not to worry because chemo is not as bad as it used to be, and medicine is improving every day.

WOW! Monday January 4, 2010 10:20 PM

Almost 3 weeks since my last entry, so much has happened, I think chemo has scared me almost as much as cancer. Tonight, I'm writing because my hair is starting to fall out. I say I'm not a hair person, but I always saw the bald heads of other people who had cancer. I guess when you look in the mirror you can't avoid knowing that you are in the battle. I guess I have to learn it's like a battle scar.

Before I started my first round of chemo, I spent 4 nights in Atlantic City. I played poker, prayed, slept, ate and enjoyed the prettiest snowstorm from the 79th floor picture in my room. The whole city was covered, it was like a picture. GOD was showing off again.

Chemo was not as bad as I had imaged. NYU cancer center has private rooms with flat screen TVs, leather lazy boys and a great staff. Vern was my chemo nurse and did not mind that I asked a lot of questions. I was there for 8 hours. Pat Henry called when she heard I had to have chemo, she told me she had to go every other week for almost three months. So far, I've had pain that I would imagine is like sickle cell pain. It feels like burning in your body because cells are being destroyed. Out of the last 13 days the pain has only been real bad 2 days, that's a real blessing. I get crazy tingling in my feet a lot, like bad frost bite, pain in my limbs but not that often. Fatigue is common and you have to learn to take naps, rest and not push your body. Chemotherapy makes it easy to get infections, so I walk with Clorox wipes, hand sanitizer, and rubber gloves. I'm very careful around people. I don't touch my face unless I wash my hands. Another thing I have learned from this is "Lord, you don't have to move that mountain, just give me the strength to climb it".

Christmas Eve was spent with Tierra, Tanya and Castel. Tierra had a little silver tree that was color-coordinated with even the wrapping paper. I had a great time watching Castel. He's such a great kid. Tanya and Tierra wrapped gifts until about 2:00 AM on Christmas morning. Christmas day, after a shower, I was so tired that I never put on my Christmas outfit. So, I wore the flowers Tierra brought me on my sweatshirt. On New Year's Eve, I went next door to Mary's to watch the ball drop. Then I suggested that we stand in a circle and tell what we were grateful for. I thanked GOD I made it into this new year cancer-free!

Craig has really been here for me, from getting my laundry done for me, getting me a TV, paying to hook cable in my room and giving me poker money (smile). It's amazing the bond you form with your children. Craig and I were growing closer but this has pushed it along with speed. Tierra shows her soft side more and more, I see the change in her.

Sunday, January 11, 2010

I shared a ride yesterday on the way to church with a lady named Barbara who is a seven-year survivor of cancer of the pancreas. I told her that she was a miracle and how blessed she was. She said she knew.

I want to tell this story about people who survived. Cancer scares us so much that we forget about the miracles.

A guy that I met told me his mother had breast cancer and the doctors told her if they didn't remove her breast she would have about six months to live. He told me that was about 20 years ago and she did not remove her breast and is still alive.

First Baptist never seems to fail me. Service yesterday was top notch, my battery gets charged every time I go. It's like the message and songs are always geared to me.

Disability is still giving me the run around; I still have not received a dime and today I almost got real stressed, but I put it in prayer and took a nap. I didn't let cancer or chemo get to me and I refused to go there about money.

Tomorrow is my first appointment with Dr. Pothuri since I started chemo. I have to go to the lab first to check my blood. Wednesday the

13th is my second round of chemo and I hope I do as well as I did the first time. Betty is coming with me to spend the day. We keep laughing and saying this will be like girl's day out talking and laughing. My hair had started breaking, so I went to Tyson's barber to cut my hair in a boy style. It looks kind of nice and everyone says so. I call it Cancer style (smile).

Tuesday, January 12, 2010

I know why I have problems with my hair falling out and looking in the mirror and seeing a bald head. I have no outward signs of cancer, so the bald head make me deal with the fact that I am in this battle, even though I'm winning.

Sitting in the doctor's waiting area at NYU Cancer Center brings into focus how many lives are affected by cancer.

Tuesday, January 12, 2010 10:00 PM

Today I had a real good visit at the Cancer Center, my numbers were good. Kathleen, my Nurse, was there and so was Dr. Pothuri.

I went into the wig shop and met with a lady named Kate (she runs the shop). Kate was like an angel from start to finish. She tried several wigs on my head, I picked a short brown one. Kate is a five-year survivor of breast cancer who got into the business of fitting patients with wigs when her friend died of breast cancer 25 years ago. Little did she know that 16 years later she would be in the battle. It amazes me that we are all coming together to fight this fight. Round 2 of chemo is tomorrow. I'm going into this round feeling very positive.

Wednesday, January 13, 2010 11:30 PM

The 2nd round of chemo did not involve as much pain as the 1st one. I think I'm more tired this time. I'm losing more hair but not my spirit. My toes are not as numb as before. It has been nine weeks since the surgery and I am able to walk a little more. I'm starting to do more things for myself. Spent a week in Atlantic City with my good friend, Yvonne, in her Timeshare. It was very relaxing and as always, we bonded.

The earthquake in Haiti and all the death and destruction puts life in its proper place. Everyone keeps telling me how my spirit is keeping me going but I don't know any other way. Sometimes I get a little scared about it coming back but then I surrender my feelings to GOD and let it go. I try to enjoy every day and every encounter because none of us know what days are our last. I'm thankful to be alive and cancer free.

Had a chance to see my fellow cancer survivor Thomasina last week, she is looking good and is still cancer free. I want to start working to have a luncheon for all my survivor friends to get together. Betty wants to have a meeting of her friends that are survivors at her house.

Wednesday, January 27, 2010 10:14 AM

I noticed that now I am wearing my bald head with pride. When I saw cancer patients with bald heads, I saw cancer, now with me I see survivor and I'm proud of all my bald community.

Thursday, January 28, 2010 10:26 PM

Today was a crazy day. A family friend for 35 years, my sister Nanette's college friend, passed away. Wanda wasn't sick as far as we know. It hit me kind of hard, life is so fragile. I can't stop thinking how blessed I am.

My friend Chris Gibson called me tonight. She is a blessing in my life, a strong prayer warrior, someone I'm glad to have on my team. GOD has a purpose for me I'm sure. He keeps putting the right people in my path. I have to stay the course with "Battle Cancer".

Tuesday, February 2, 2010 8:27 PM

Round three for chemo! Now that I look back, the chemo that I was so afraid of is almost over, thank GOD, and it was not as bad as I imagine. I realized that there are many people that have chemo every week and some have it for years. I'm really blessed. The devil tries to tell me that it's not over and it can come back. I don't plan to live in fear of cancer. I plan to live my life. 90 days ago my life was turned upside down and now it's time to set it right side up again. Back to losing weight, taking care of myself, take stress out of the picture and get going with my mission for Battle Cancer. I get kind of emotional knowing this journey takes me on new steps.

I'm a little disappointed with Rosie, she called me to tell me she can't make it to my chemo. Maybe GOD wanted me to take this last step with just him (smile). I'm glad to know that today is my last day of chemo, no matter what the devil says. I've come this far by faith.

On my way to the Veteran's Administration for my pills. 2 pills = $388 in the drug store -- $0 at the VA. It's sad that medicine to save or improve your life could cost so much.

Met a woman on the ride over that had two battles with breast cancer. She is 87 years old. Her last battle was when she was 82. I told her I want to live to 87 and tell my story.

Wednesday, February 3, 2010 9:09 AM

Just saw Dr. Pothuri. I am doing well and I don't have to come back for 3 months. Then every six months for five years. Then once a year. Had a cuff test today (internal exam). Everything looks good. I can exercise, take baths and have sex.

Friday, February 5, 2010 7:53 AM

Day two after my last chemo… Last night I had the burning in my pubic area but I didn't take the pain medicine. This morning the burning sensation was in my whole body. Still didn't take the medicine. Spoke to Rosie yesterday and told her how I felt about her calling me at the last minute. She said she will make it up to me and she wants to learn how to speak her mind like me with love. She knows I don't say anything about my friends until I tell them first. Cancer survivors don't need stress (not that anyone does) and at 61 I'm going to nip stress in the butt. I have already surrendered stress to GOD.

Saturday, February 6, 2010 8:14 AM

I don't remember the pain this bad with chemo round 2, but no pain no gain. I woke up this morning at 12:30 am and took those pain pills and might have to take another one after I eat.

Thursday, February 11, 2010 3:00 PM

This round of chemo must have been the most painful. Saturday and Sunday the 6th and the 7th I slept most of the day. The burning sensation and the fatigue were more than I can remember from before. Maybe because my system is filled with the chemo, it's breaking my body down. I only pray for the people who go through this every week with no end in sight. I pray for the ones that need chemo to continue to live. I thank GOD for the blessing that I only had to have 3 sessions and it's over. I have to stay on course and get my life back so that I can go on to do great work with Battle Cancer. I have to lift others spirits like GOD has lifted mine. I know that I would have never made this journey without strong faith. The battle has been much easier with faith and the support of my children and friends.

Just came back to my hotel room after playing poker, I love the game. The people here really like and respect me and the ones who know the battle that I've been through show so much concern in their eyes.

GOD has blessed me with good spirits and it shows. I have to pass this spirit around. I wear my bald head proud even in the poker room. Everyone has someone in their life that has been affected. People tell me their stories. They tell me about diet, vitamins, treatments and how they are praying for me.

Friday, February 12, 2010 4:32 PM

I felt so full today in the poker room. They have a picture of a young female dealer who has been fighting brain cancer for about 2 years, a young mother who is now in a hospice. They took the picture down, of a dealer who lost his battle about a month ago. I realize how blessed I am and never want to take it or life for granted. I never want to believe that it will come back.

Monday, February 15, 2010 5:59 AM

What a life, I just spent the best Valentine day of my life. No flowers, no candy, no cards, no call from a husband. I spent the day giving and receiving a lot of love. "I love you" echoed all day from me and from everyone I spoke to. I spent the day with my grandson and 4 of my five children, and a nephew that I love.

I met a woman today that might be the mother of future grandchildren and I know that I'm going to love her. She is pretty smart and loves my son. She laughed while my children shared memories of their childhood. This was Tyson's first visit since cancer struck, after the hug he told me not to cry. I showed him my bald head and he loves it. My children don't like the wig. They like the head bald and proud. Tanya tried to style the wig while I tried different earrings (smile). I feel so loved and I thank GOD my children are grown. I can't image having small children going through this, but people battle cancer every day and have small children. Look how blessed I am.

Wednesday, February 17, 2010 8:31 AM

Yesterday was 13 days since the last round of chemo but this time the pain seems worse. Numbness is still around. It's mostly on the left side. I had a funny sharp pain on the right side of my pelvic area. That pain was kind of shooting. I found out last week that my Aunt Cynthia's husband, Robert, died of stomach cancer 5 years ago. I knew he had problems with his stomach, but I didn't know it was cancer. My aunt told me that the doctors gave him 2 years, but he only lived 1 year. She said he said he wanted to die because he was in so much pain. She said that he didn't really want to have treatment, so he went faster. I believe that your spirit has a lot to do with what happens also.

Friday, February 19, 2010 11:25 AM

I have been spending the last four days with Castel, my 6-year-old grandson, spending time and talking with him is such a blessing, I always enjoy him on our vacations together but now it's even more special. This is what life is all about, making memories. My good friend Denise died from cancer 14 days before her first grandchild was born. So I know what a blessing this is.

Monday, February 22, 2010 8:53 AM

Yesterday a woman that I know named Judith, who has been fighting throat cancer for about 8-10 years, was found dead in her apartment. She was a wonderful woman who did not let cancer slow her down from living, even when it came back twice. Our last conversation was before I found out about mine. We lost contact about a year ago. She is another example of living and surviving cancer. This time I seem to be having more problems with neuropathy in my feet and my left hand. A woman at church told me that a friend of hers completed Chemo 2 years ago and still has neuropathy. I know it's still better than having cancer.

Wednesday, February 24, 2010

It's been 3 weeks since my last chemo and this is the first time since November 22, 2009 that I don't have a doctor's appointment. (yeah). Called my job today to see about going back to work, Aida said they will get back to me.

Monday, March 1, 2010 12:40 PM

This weekend I found out that two of the men that I play poker with are cancer survivors. One had prostate cancer 19 years ago and the other had a tumor on his right hip over a year ago. It's funny how people will tell you their stories when you have something in common with them. The one who is the 19-year survivor I've known for about 10 years and this is the first time I heard his story. There are a lot of stories in the poker room. We need to have a fund raiser.

Wednesday, March 10, 2010 1:45 PM

Today at the VA hospital I was talking to a man when I was online about cancer and he told me his wife died of cancer. I saw him later in the cafeteria and when I went to the cashier to pay for my breakfast the cashier told me that my meal was paid for by the man who was talking to me.

Saturday, March 20, 2010 12:50 PM

The underdog can win, because the bumble bee can fly. We all know the weight of the bee's body and the weight of the winds should make it impossible for her to fly but no one has told the bee that. I try to tell myself every day that the battle takes me closer to my goals and where

GOD needs me to be. I'm having funny pains in my body and I notice it happens when I eat wheat or have indigestion. I have a lot of doctors, so I plan to ask a lot of questions.

Tuesday, March 23, 2010

Three doctor appointments in two days. The heart monitor came off today. I wore it for 24 hours. It wasn't so bad. My blood work came back and results are good. I spoke to the doctor about the modular on my lungs and the fear I have about it. The funny thing is that after I went to church on Sunday, I really haven't had that much fear or given it much thought. Rev. Norman also spoke about things in our lives, good and bad, that prepare us for where we need to be. I was broke and the devil told me not to tithe my last $20. But I did anyway and my cousin Denise put a bill in my hand. She told me if I didn't take it, she would be mad with me. When I got home it was a hundred-dollar bill, she might not have known how broke I was, but GOD did.

Saturday, March 27, 2010 6:42 PM

Just came home from Wanda Young's memorial, she wasn't sick, but died 2 days after getting food poisoning. The last time I saw her was the day after I found out that I had cancer November 3, 2009 at Marissa's services (died after a 2-year battle with stomach cancer). I guess Wanda's work on earth was done.

I got good news on Thursday. The CAT scan on my lungs showed 2 modules but they are calcium and not malignant. I have to have a CAT scan every 3 months. The heart monitor test results have not come back yet. Everyone told me at Wanda's service how good I looked, and Anita

Burson said she's been praying for me. I told her to keep on and thanks, I like her spirit. My fuzzy hair is starting to grow back, Tierra noticed this week. Wednesday will be 8 weeks since my last chemo and I cannot believe it. My body is starting to feel better, but I still try to rest a lot. I don't think I'm going back to work. I plan to call Social Security Monday and get- the-ball-rolling…another turning point in my life. I know that every day I try to enjoy as much life as I can. I try not to take any of this for granted. I humble myself in a lot of ways. I am more selective about whom I spend my time with and I'm more to myself. My daughter, Tierra, and I are bonding like never before, a good relationship is turning into a great one. I still say that this journey has been a blessing for me. It's like taking baby steps into a new life. Pastor White once preached about the 2nd mile of life. The Lord is blessing me right now.

Monday, March 29, 2010 9:38 AM

I keep meeting cancer survivors. Yesterday my Access-a-Ride driver told me he has colon cancer. He said that he has never been sick before this. His blood count was so low that he had to have 2 pints of blood. They sent him for an MRI which showed that he had a tumor that tested positive for cancer. They cut away part of his colon. He gets chemo once a week for a year. We talk about staying healthy, eating right and how cancer is such a scary road to go down. I told him that we were blessed to be able to share our story. I called Social Security this morning to start my paperwork. I'm ready to leave my job and spend my days doing what makes me happy.Sunday, April 4, 2010

Happy Easter, I went to sunrise service this morning at 6 AM. I couldn't sleep last night because I didn't want to oversleep. Well the service was well worth it. This has been a great week, Wednesday the 31st was 8 weeks since my last chemo and I am feeling good. Thank GOD. Friday the 2nd (Good Friday) was 5 months since the cancer battle started and I am still winning, thank GOD again.

I spent 4 days and 3 nights with Castel and the Gietschier family. We spent it in A/C (Atlantic City) with adjoining rooms. I have not spent time with them (the Gietschier family) on vacation in about 5 years. We spent a lot of time together. I treasure all the moments like this even more since I became a cancer survivor.

The lady in the wig shop in NYU told me that because of her breast cancer, some of her friends stopped calling her and acted like cancer was something they could catch. I have been so blessed my friends have become even better, closer and more there for me than they were before. Today I'm going to have Easter dinner with the Leslie family. I have known them over 20 years and the friendship gets better each year. Thank GOD.

Wednesday, April 7, 2010 8:27 AM

My sister is a 7-year breast cancer survivor and lately she has been having headaches and numbness in her legs. She doesn't have medical coverage because of a pre-existing condition. She came to New York and went to the emergency room at Kings County hospital. They kept her to run tests. That was yesterday. Another cancer survivor that I know had a biopsy 2 weeks ago and they found a walnut size tumor (cancer). He has to go for radiation shots for the next 5 weeks so they can shrink it. Then remove it with surgery. I'm sure that all cancer survivors must think about this and dread this kind of news. This is all new to me but if I don't feel right or get any kind of pain, I start to wonder. Keep praying Rosalind, keep praying.

There is a lady I know whose husband's leg broke while he was standing up. They rushed him to the hospital. After taking tests they found out that he had stage 4 lung cancer that had spread to his bones. They told him to go home and get his life in order. He lived 9 more months.

I enjoy life and people, every morning I awake I thank GOD. I tell people how dear they are to me and show it with my actions. Today, my sister Irene is having a biopsy on a tumor that they found in her brain. I'm praying for her, like so many people did and are doing for me. When I went for my biopsy October 2009, cancer was not even on my mind, now it is every day. My sister is already saying that if it is cancer, she does not want chemo or radiation. She says she wants to go home to her house on the lake if her time is limited. Life is a battle sometimes, but we have to wait and pray. It looks like another family member might be battling again but I pray that she doesn't have to. My advice -- don't claim it until you have to.

Monday, April 12, 2010 10:05 AM

"By our spirit and our blessing, we are healed". Another friend is 83 years old. He is a 15-year survivor of lung cancer. They found a small spot when he had a regular chest x-ray 7 years ago.

It moved to his bladder. He got treatment and so far, so good.

Tuesday, April 13, 2010 9:24 AM

I just found out what I think I already knew. My sister has cancer again. It's in her neck, brain and in her bones. She says she doesn't want chemo, but she might have radiation. When I started this journal, I never imagine it would lead to all this. My mother does not know that it has spread. I really feel sorry for her. This is her third time around dealing with her children's cancer. I told my sister Nanette that I saw a story about a family in "People" magazine where 3 sisters were going through chemo at the same time.

My hair is starting out as a little fuzz and now my sister has cancer again. Today will be my first visit to see her. The visit will make it real, because right now it feels like a nightmare.

Wednesday, April 14, 2010 9:22 PM

Went to visit my sister yesterday at the hospital. She has double vision in her left eye, and she says that she has pain in her torso. The doctors gave her a shot of morphine. Tonight at 8:30 my sister Nanette told me that Irene is terminal with about 6 to 12 months to live. I really don't think the way her health is going down she will make it that long. I can't believe that I'm writing this. I think that I'm in shock. This cancer is a bad scare. Now I'm wondering if it will come back, where will it come back and how long from now? The plan is to give my sister radiation 5 times a week for 6 weeks. She wants to go to her house on Lake Michigan to enjoy her remaining time. Funny thing about cancer is that doctors give you a time, but someone will leave their house today and not come home. They won't even have a warning. I'm asking GOD to be with us as we take this journey with my sister who is a Mother, a daughter and aunt. I'm really numb, I don't know how I really feel.

Sunday, April 18, 2010 10:10 PM

I look in the mirror now and see the cute gray fuzz that is starting to cover my head. It makes me happy and proud that the battle has been won. I just have to stay positive. The last few days I have had to battle the devil because of my feelings about my sister's cancer coming back. Now when the fears come, I say I am healed.

Friday, April 23, 2010 1:45 PM

SMOG...last night I had a weird dream. There was this small cloud of smog that was attacking people and when it got on them, they would fall and die. I kept running from this cloud in my dream. As I ran, I warned people about it. When I woke up this morning, I told myself that the cloud of smog was cancer.

Monday, April 26, 2010 4:20 PM

My sister Irene has some sort of disorder that is a side effect of breast cancer. My sister Nanette informed me that the disorder also comes (or is a result) of other cancers. I want to find out the name so that when I go to Dr. Pothuri I can ask her about it. The doctors are saying that it is not just this cancer that is killing her but the results of the breast cancer from seven years ago. My sister has lost the use of her legs and has about 8 or more sessions of radiation. She does not want them to stick a needle in her head to biopsy her brain. She is still in good spirits (I am told). Her body is starting to break down, we still can pray for a miracle.

Tuesday, April 27, 2010 11:17 PM

My sister has neoplastic meningitis (that's the easy word for it). They don't know how long she has had it because she just went to doctor three weeks ago. Yesterday they told her that they are going to do physical therapy and the family should start looking for a hospice. I can't imagine being told there is no hope. 10 years ago, this Saturday, May 1st, my father lost a 12-year battle with lung cancer. It's hard to believe I'm living this again. Knowing that I just battled cancer myself makes it so hard. I'm going to the hospital to see her tomorrow, but I don't want her to see me cry.

Thursday, April 29, 2010 8:25 PM

I really don't feel well these days. My mind gets busy with things. I went to see my sister yesterday her spirit is good. Since my last visit 10 days ago, she lost the use of her legs and bladder. The nurses tried to get her on her on feet but couldn't. She drank a little water and some fish broth but really not eating. My sisters are getting ready to bring her home to Nanette's house where she can use the first floor. She will need a hospital bed and a full-time home attendant. Nanette retired in July 2009 and since then she has dealt with two terminal cases of cancer, her close friend and now her sister. My sister, Irene (my mother's name), is battling cancer 28 years after her name sake lost her battle. My mother stated this morning that before she has to watch my sister become skin and bones, she would rather not go see her. Funny in life we don't get that choice. As a mother we watch our children come into this world and sadly some of us have to watch them leave. Yesterday I watched a nurse put boots on my sister to strengthen her ankles. I can't imagine what kind of things are going through her head at the moment.

Monday, May 3, 2010 10:57 AM

Yesterday marked 6 months since I found out that I had cancer. This sure has been a ride, but a ride with more highs than lows. I found out that my friends are really my friends; that some family members value material things and money more then they value people. I found out that my children are grown people and their father, and I did a pretty good job with them. I couldn't be getting better care from them. I found out what's important in life; that my 7-year-old grandson telling me he wants me to live with him because I'm fun is special. He also told me that he didn't mind helping me to put on my shoes when I was sick. I found out that my sisters-in-law (the Cox family) love and respect me no matter when they see me. (I never really left the sisters). I found out that I don't have to try to fit into anyone else's life. They should be trying to fit into mine. I found out what it really means to have grace from the Lord. I found out that a great spirit is better than money. I found out that a kind word or deed can open more doors than I could have imagined. I found out that I am loved more than I knew. I found out that it is great being me. I found out that when you find out who you are, you won't want to be anyone else. This had been a journey that I'm glad that I didn't have to take alone. I found out that time is a blessing and that I want to spend it being happy, with people I love and who love me. I found out that it's okay to be scared and talk about it. I found out that it's okay to ask for help. I found out its okay to laugh, cry, and take naps in the middle of the day. I found out that it's okay to smile when I see a baby (life goes on).

I found out that there are many cancer stories out there with many survivors. I found out that GOD has blessed me with a network of them. In the next few weeks, months, years I will get on with my life. I may have to watch my sister lose her 2nd battle with cancer, but I told my friend Lavern (at church yesterday) I still believe in miracles.

Tuesday, May 4, 2010 11:08 AM

I'm trying to lose weight, so I decided to walk around the neighborhood. Tonight, I ran into an old neighbor named Hyacinth, who used to work at Sloan Kettering. We spoke for about 40 minutes. We talked about our children, grandchildren and about things that went on the last 22 years since we were neighbors. She told me how great it was that my cancer was found early because uterine cancer is hard to detect in the early stages. She said it doesn't show up in most pap smears. I told her that Dr. Friedman was a blessing and a humble human being. He had said he was not a cancer specialist and wanted me to go to a doctor that specialized in cancer care. Hyacinth also told me that she understood me not going to the hospital a lot to see my sister. She told me to call my sister and encourage her, so I plan to do that.

Thursday, May 6, 2010 6:22 PM

Yesterday was my first 90-day checkup with Nurse Lutz and Dr. Pothuri. Everything went well. All my tests (internal and external) look good and I'm healing well. Thanks GOD. I spoke to them about my sister. They both listened and understood how I must feel. Adama Maitland, the assistant nurse, told me that the last two months at the cancer center were tough. She said one case hit her pretty bad. A woman named Nadia was the same age as she is (in their twenties). Adama had to take a few days off to deal with it. This cancer is a crazy ride. Today was breast clinic for me, the cyst in my left breast has grown and Dr. Wade wants to remove it. She and the head radiation director looked at the film and decided that it should be removed. Neither of them believes that it's cancer but they don't want to take any chances. I feel comfortable that it's not. My daughter, Tanya, just had one removed and she will take me on May 27th. It will be in and out. Thanks GOD. Dr. Wade just wants to be sure, because my sister had breast cancer. My sister has lost 30lbs in 30 days. My sister, Mary said that she is starting to look like our grandmother who lost her battle 27 years ago. I don't want to see her this way, but I have no choice. I still believe in miracles.

Tuesday, May 11, 2010 8:59 AM

Sunday was Mother's Day and I went with my mother and my sister, Nanette, to their church. After church we went to see my sister Irene. She amazes me every time I see her, she has a great spirit and it must be hard. Last week on the news they reported that one in five women would get cancer, out of four sister two of us have had to battle. It might be about our genes, but I believe that it has a lot to do with the environment also. My sister's head is dark from the radiation, her feet are swollen and she can't use her legs. She has no control of her bladder and she has lost most of her vision. I plan to go to the hospital more to see her. Everyone wants to know if I can handle it. My reply is if this is the end of her life, I will spend the time with her anyway I can. Irene is in pain and she gets chills like I use to after chemo. When I saw her bald head Sunday, I told her that she was trying to wear her hair like mine, she smiled (still has her sense of humor). When I walk around the park now and get tired, I remember that she said she wants to walk out of the hospital just like she walked in. I still believe in miracles.

Saturday, May 29, 2010

WOW I have been missing in action! Not really. I just ran away and took a break from all that's going on. Since my last writing, my sister has been moved to a rehab center and the radiation has stopped. Her son said that this place is better for her because, it teaches her how to live. She wears her own clothes and not a gown during the day. She looks good because she is dressed nice. She gets therapy every day in some form and her spirits are good. There are times when she cries (we all do). My sister Nanette gave her a Journal, but she only has one pound of pressure in her hand and cannot write. I plan to go once a week and write for her. I went early last Saturday. We were able to talk one-on-one and it was a blessing. We spent two and a half hours alone. We talked about so much, she told me that she will never see a grandchild, I told her why I didn't come to the hospital often and she understood.

When you never had cancer, you hardly hear the word. When you have had the battle, it's like having a gray car, you notice all the gray cars. My friend Rose told me about a lady in her church that had breast cancer after she had her breast removed. She started taking chemo again, had a bad reaction and now she is in a coma. You hear so many stories, that at times your head starts to spin. My friend Pat (who is a 1-year survivor) took a CAT scan. They saw 2 spots on her lungs. Now we are praying on that. She is getting ready to take a bone scan. This is the first time I have noticed fear in her voice. I take another scan on my lungs in 19 days, my left ankle is sore and swollen and I don't know what's up with that. I go to the VA on Wednesday, so I will ask someone to look at my ankle hopefully something bit me (smile).

I met a man the other day that had a heart transplant, then got skin cancer and survived. I told him that he is double blessed. I know one thing -- I'm really enjoying life more (even with less money). I value loved ones even more than before and I realize how blessed I am every day.

Thursday, June 3, 2010 10:12 AM

4 months since my last chemo. I'm feeling really blessed. I've heard so many stories of other people's battles that did not end as well as mine. A cousin named Karen that lives in Maryland, that I baby sat and remember when she was born, is now in her forties. She is dying from stage 4 colon cancer. She never had a colonoscopy, because she wasn't fifty yet. I had a colonoscopy, they found 4 polyps. The doctors told me to call in 2 weeks for the results, but I know it's nothing and I'm not worried. It's all in GOD'S hands anyway. I am going to see my sister Irene who I haven't seen in 12 days. I hear that she lost more pressure in her hands and that the cancer is slowly moving up her spine. I notice in my journey that I am getting so much better with needles and procedures, it's like it's becoming a part of my life. I feel bless to have medical care and great doctors that follow-up with me.

Today a nurse called to see if I was in any pain after one procedure, I told her thanks I'm doing well. My friend Yvonne went with me yesterday, she is another blessing in my life. This is when you know who your friends are.

Thursday, June 3, 2010 10:39 PM

Spoke to Pat Henry today, we spoke about our different tests and about our birthdays coming up. Her birthday is the 10th and mine is the 14th. We plan to forget cancer for those days and celebrate life. I was just thinking that I have a cyst in my breast and polyps have to be removed from my colon. It kind of scares me a little knowing that all these things have to be biopsied. I pray and believe that everything is negative but every now and then the mind wonders so, I keep telling myself that I am healed.

Sunday, June 6, 2010 12:29 AM

My Mother just left my room, she was sitting with her head hanging down, she has been hanging her head since she saw my sister on Friday. It can't be an easy cross to bear, we give birth to our children, but we don't expect to see their life slip away.

Monday, June 7, 2010 9:07 AM

I just came back from the park exercising. It's a group that I started and stopped with over the last 6 years. This was the first day post-cancer. I use to take this class like a breeze, but today I was out of breath half way into it. I started to quit, then a small voice called my name, I smiled and kept on going I said, "Okay, Irene I'll do it for you". She has not been able to use her legs for about 6 weeks now and is slowly losing the use of her hands. Someone has to start feeding her, this is the sister that used to walk 5 miles a day and drive for hours without stopping, among other activities.

Tuesday, June 8, 2010 6:07 PM

Today I fed my sister. Brushed her teeth and tongue. Then took her outside in her wheelchair for some air. There is a beautiful garden at the rehab center. My beautiful sister, the independent author who now fights to use her hands. This is the first day I broke down in front of her. God have mercy on her please. I know that he has mercy but I'm just praying for a little more. No one knows how she feels having her body shut down on her.

Tuesday, June 8, 2010 9:56 PM

Just got back from my first choir rehearsal. Really found my home at First Baptist.

Thursday, June 10, 2010 8:49 AM

Cancer has given me life! Anyone who knows me knows that I enjoy life but now I enjoy it even more. I really try to enjoy each moment. I really stop and smell the flowers, enjoy the sky, enjoy people and all the events of the day no matter good or bad. Everything in life is not pleasant but there is joy in everything. I can't see a baby now without smiling with joy, life must go on.

Saturday, June 12, 2010 9:39 AM

Everyone is trying to hold up, but the mood is getting kind of somber around here. We are watching cancer destroy a loved one again. My sister's body is turning against her while we sit by helplessly and watch. We try to make sure that someone is always there to feed her. She still has her smile and sense of humor, but you can see the fear in her eyes. Her legs are starting to turn in. She has no control of her motor skills and she thanks you for every little thing that you do for her. We are slowing losing her while we try to mend our hearts and lives. When I go to the nursing home, I thank GOD for my healing. I think this could have been me (sometimes I think will it be me). By GOD'S grace it's not me and I keep moving on. It is becoming a blessing helping to care for her (it is a blessing to give than receive).

Saturday, June 12, 2010 9:45 PM

I wasn't able to feed my sister today, she was rushed to the hospital today because, they could not put a Foley bag in her and she was in extreme pain.

Monday, June 14, 2010 2:30 PM

Happy Birthday to me! My first birthday since CANCER! American Cancer Society says "we're in the business of more birthdays" and boy do I feel blessed. June has become my official Month of one big celebration. I have mini vacations, dinners, parties, a play and spending time with loved ones planned.

Friday, June 18, 2010 9:16 AM

Today on TV one of the feature stories was about 2 sisters fighting breast cancer together. Their Father died from cancer and 2 of their aunts had it. I listened because I realize now how all the information I get about cancer helps with the fight and because I have daughters, nieces and cousins. Yesterday I went to the breast clinic for an appointment. There was a man in the waiting room with his wife. I later found out that he was there because he had breast cancer. He is not the regular face of breast cancer, but he is the face. Today I also got the results of my colonoscopy (negative). The devil tried to make me crazy while I waited for the results. I kept telling myself that I was healed and thank GOD I am. I told everyone that I spoke to the good news.

Now on to my birthday celebrations! My sister is doing much better than last Saturday. She is still in the hospital, but the infection is under control and they have increased her morphine to help with the pain.

Sunday, June 20, 2010 11:08 PM

I feel really blessed. I just have to say, with all that is going on; I must take time to say how blessed and loved I feel. I really enjoy my days and most of the people around me. I was blessed this week to see Betty retire after knowing her for over 50 years. I went to a 75th birthday party for Monica who is full of life, we both danced until we were tired. I had dinner with two breast cancer survivors (Pat and Dorothy). So many amazing people are in my life, if you want to know how rich you are, think of all the things you have that money can't buy!

Monday, June 21, 2010 10:19 PM

Had dinner with Pat Henry (uterine cancer survivor). We celebrated our birthdays - her 2nd since cancer - my 1st. It's great to have a friend that understands what you went and are going through. She is having a hard time with medical coverage. If she was unemployed, she could get

Medicaid, but she can't live off the little bit of money. Pat has worked all of her life and now that she has cancer the system is punishing her.

Tuesday, June 29, 2010 9:45 PM

Just had my 2nd doctor's appointment for the week, with 3 more to go. The modules in my lung are not getting any bigger, Thank GOD! No more scan needed for 6 months. Dr. Stern wants ENT to look at my Thyroid and then look at the spot on my Pancreas. Oh well I know that I'm healed and I feel good. Most of my family is going on a cruise Saturday (my sisters and their families, not my children). I plan to visit my sister Irene more while they are away, but I realize that I can't run myself down, so I will do the best I can. Dr. Stein said that she doesn't think that my swollen ankles are anything, she said just elevate my legs as much as possible. She said she doesn't understand where all these modules are coming from in my body; well as long as they don't turn into anything, I'm okay.

Wednesday, June 30, 2010 8:31 AM

Today after waking up and thanking GOD, I said to myself, "Life always has its valleys and peaks". Right now, I am going through a peak, I don't want to worry about tomorrow, I want to enjoy today.

Thursday, July 1, 2010 8:17 AM

Spoke to Mrs. Christian this morning (my Mother's friend). She is a 23-year Breast cancer survivor. I told her that I'm praying and staying positive so that I can make 23 years like her. We talk about GOD and faith (real faith). It was a blessing to talk to someone who loves GOD and has survived the battle for 23 years.

Wednesday, July 7, 2010 8:46 AM

My sister Irene called at 7:24 a.m. this morning to tell me she needs me at the hospital right away. She wants to be moved and spoke to our cousin Jeanette about it. I really think that she is starting to have moments without clarity. I spent 7 hours with her on Saturday. My sisters are not here and the only ones here are my brother Tommy and myself. I want to go but I'm tired and I know what she wants is not an emergency. I feel bad but I can't make it right away. She told me Saturday that she is trying to hold on until the family comes back from the cruise. I told her to let go and go to GOD whenever she feels the need.

Friday at the VA they told me that I have spots on my pancreas and my thyroid. I have to have a sonogram of my throat. I spoke to a woman name Anita and she told me that all the little modules etc. showing up are little parts of my body that are trying to heal themselves. She said that my body has taken a hit and it's trying to get itself back together. That sounds like the best reason I've heard for all these breakouts. I spoke to another uterine cancer survivor today and we talked about sex after cancer. I wonder will if it hurt? Will I bleed? Does it have anything to do with it coming back? I believe when the time comes, I will be fine but I still wonder.

Wednesday, July 7, 2010 10:30 AM

Today is the 101st birthday of my grandmother, Irene Munroe, who died 27 ½ years ago from cancer. My sister had a bad day yesterday. She doesn't want to be alone and while there I noticed that she was twisting her nose. I realized that she couldn't scratch her nose, so I did it for her. It humbles you to know that there are so many things that we take for granted in life.

It's record breaking temperatures and I only have a ceiling fan and it's starting to tire me out. I'm taking it kind of easy as much as I can. My sister called me to come back to the hospital again today, but I just couldn't make it. Dr. Webb (breast surgeon) called and my surgery is scheduled for July 15th (my son Craig's 41st birthday). A mass of negative tissues is what she will be taking out. I've come this far by faith and I won't turn around now.

Monday, July 12, 2010 12:18 AM

In less than 48 hours I will be having breast surgery. I can't believe what I been going through the last 81/2 months, but I'm still coming out on the right side of the mountain. I pray real hard that this mass in my breast is negative. I've been passing all my tests with good results and I'm believing that it will continue. My daughter, Tierra, will go with me to the hospital. Thank GOD for children.

Friday, July 16, 2010 1:01 AM

Yesterday was my surgery and I think it went well. First, they put a wire in my breast (because the mass was so small). Then they took me to surgery and the mass was removed. I came home with a Penrose drain in my breast to help with the healing and drainage of the wound. They use an instrument like a safety pin on the head of the drain so that they can pull it out in 5 days. My next appointment with Dr. Webb is July 29th. I feel safe and confident with her and her team. I have been blessed with great doctors through this journey. Now I have to wait for the results of the biopsy. I believe that everything will be negative.

I'm proud of Tierra. She was a real trooper again yesterday.

Monday, July 19, 2010 11:12 AM

I'm on my way to the emergency room to see about this drain. Yesterday Betty looked at it in church and said that too much was going on with it so, I should let a doctor look at it. I can't wait to take a shower when this drain is removed. It's amazing what you think about when you are dealing with cancer. Saw my sister Irene today and I am amazed that she is still alive. I whispered in her ear to go home to GOD. The other day she told me she wants to stop taking the medicine because its keep her from being able to walk out of the hospital. The cancer is really affecting her brain now.

Monday, July 19, 2010 5:15 PM

Back from the hospital, the surgeon on call told me that I should have changed the dressing. The pad smelled like old blood and it was drenched. Dr. Alaverz changed the dressing, gave me tape and pads and told me that I could take a shower. Everything is looking good and I should have the results in about 7-10 days. I'm feeling good about it and the drain comes out in 8 days.

Wednesday, July 28, 2010 12:13 AM

I texted and called everyone in my circle to tell them the good news that I received. No cancer in the mass at all! Such positive feed-back!

Today Pat Henry has a CAT scan. As always, my cancer survivor friend is in my prayers and the journey continues. I found out today that Dr. Ryan (one of my thyroid doctors) was on the team of doctors that admitted and worked on my sister the first few weeks when she was in Kings County. He said the case had them baffled because she walked into the emergency room and went downhill from there and so fast. It's important for cancer survivors to do medical follow-ups (which most of the time she didn't). The second-best thing I heard today was when Dr. Webb told me see you next year!

Saturday, July 31, 2010 11:04 AM

Life is wonderful and my plans to enjoy every day are working - from walking in the morning and thanking GOD for every new day to enjoying the birds in the backyard who sing so beautiful early in the morning. Those birds know that GOD will take care of them and they don't worry about what the day will bring. They do what they do best - they sing. I plan to do what I do best, live and share gifts without worry. Wednesday, I spent the day with Betty and her granddaughter Asia (age 14 ½). We shopped, laughed, shared and bonded. Friday, I spent the day with Yvonne doing things we never did before. We have been friends over 20 years. We went to Trader Joe's for health food, followed by a bar on Court Street for lunch (no drinks). Then we went to a day spa for manicures and pedicures. What a blessing this week has been, good news and good friends. I have been trying to text positive messages to friends every day and say something positive to a stranger, I'm loving life.

Sunday, August 1, 2010 5:01 PM

Had a wonderful time in church today. Then I went to see my sister in the nursing home. She barely spoke to me and she is getting so thin. She is not even drinking water and she isn't on any kind of drip. She is weak but tries to smile. I keep telling her to let go and go to GOD. A lady that volunteers in the home brought a portable keyboard to the room. I sang some gospel songs while she played. It was a beautiful experience that I will remember all my life. Thank you, GOD for another blessing.

Monday, August 2, 2010 8:58 PM

Today I had a biopsy of my thyroid. That was different having a needle in and out of my neck for a series of five sets. I was awake but it was done with local anesthesia. As always, I had a great team working on me. It's strange that Dr. Ryan worked on the team. He's the same doctor that worked on my sister almost 4 months ago. I have to wait 15 days for the results. I trust and believe that it will be negative.

Thursday, August 5, 2010 12:10 PM

Saw Dr. Pothuri today along with Kathleen Lutz (my nurse practitioner). Everything looks good - waiting for the blood results. They want me to have a bone density test.

My friend Pat Henry had a CAT scan of her lungs and received the report today. Her modules in her lungs have grown in the last two months. She might need another biopsy on her lungs. I told her it will be negative and that we have to stay in prayer. I know this journey with cancer can have its ups and downs.

My friend's cousin felt a lump in her breast January this year. She had a sonogram and they told her it was nothing. Six months later she has stage 2 breast cancer and is going through chemo for six weeks now. Cancer touches everyone. My aunt's 82-year-old friend died about 3 weeks after they found out that she had ovarian cancer. The battle continues every day for someone. On October 17th I want to walk in Prospect Park Walk for the Cure. I would like to go with a group to raise money.

Thursday, August 5, 2010 6:46 PM

I'm looking at the news and it seems like every hour someone is talking about the battle with cancer. I don't know if it's because the word is so loud to me now or if it's being talked about more and more.

Thursday, August 12, 2010 11:25 PM

On the Today show they talked about a member of the staff that passed away at age 60 from ovarian cancer. They said she fought a good battle and seem like she was getting better. Tears rolled down my face, I didn't know her, but this battle affects us all. Yesterday Lou Ann, a worker at Taj Mahal, told me she has to have brain surgery again. Her tumor grew back, it was negative before and it only grows back in 10 percent of the patients. I told her that I would pray for her and that she has to believe that she is healed. I have results that I'm waiting on but I hardly think about it because I believe that I am healed. My Mother said yesterday that my sister is slipping more and more, and it might not be long. She has been hanging in there for some time, but it still seems unreal.

Saturday, August 14, 2010 11:34 AM

Going home today from Atlantic City. Royce from NYU will call me on Tuesday to talk about an article that will be on the NYU Robotic surgery website on the surgery that I had in November. I'm looking forward to that.

My sister is still holding on.

Two people that I know from playing poker just had cancer surgery (hip and prostrate). It looks like every hour you hear about somebody with cancer. In three days I will get the results from my thyroid biopsy. I know that I'm healed. Lately I'm really into medical shows, it amazes me how man's knowledge can go into the human body and a little procedure can tell what's going on inside. My friend has nodules that are growing on her lungs (I have modules on my lungs) Her nodules are getting bigger. They want to go into her lungs and biopsy them. Her son is coming to NY while she is in the hospital overnight, she asked me to pray for her, I always do.

Monday, August 15, 2010 10:21 AM

My sister lost her battle with cancer at 6:30 pm on 8/14/2010 - 55 years and 6 months after her birth. She was surrounded by family and friends when she took her last breath in peace. I was on my way back from NJ and my mother and sister were on their way back from Connecticut. My soul feels broken, my sister is gone, and my friend Pat has to have lung surgery.

I did not make it to church today and I'm trying to find peace. We knew that the end was coming for my sister but now it doesn't seem real. My journal has bible readings for each day and today is Proverb 3:5. "Trust in the Lord with all thine heart and lean not unto thine own understanding". Great words for me today! Thank You GOD, you're always looking out for me.

Wednesday, August 17, 2010 10:01 AM

I can't say we are in shock, but I will say we are numb. We have been blessed (my mother's direct line) has not had a funeral in almost 28 years. My sister's body is still in the morgue, we are waiting for her son Chris to come in from LA. I have spent more time in the last 48 hours with my sisters than I have spent with them in the last year. I guess when the chain is broken the remaining links get stronger (we will see).

I have a doctor's appointment at 3 p.m. for the results of my thyroid biopsy. My son Tyson is flying in to see me this weekend. It's been six months since I've seen him. I believe he is coming to see me because of Pat's new lung surgery and my sister's condition (he made these plans before she passed).

Tuesday, August 17, 2010 1:19 PM

Just received a call from the pathology department at the VA. The results from the procedure when they went down my throat show a little bit of abnormalities. They want me to make sure that I keep up with my appointments. They will repeat the procedure again in 9-12 months because these growths can turn into cancer. GOD is still with me and as the song says, "for the rest of my life I will trust him".

Now for some good news - the tissue from my thyroid shows no cancer cells whatsoever. The same song says, "he been good to me". One more test and we are home free.

Wednesday, August 18, 2010 10:11 PM

I have to have a CAT-scan on my pancreas. There seems to be a lesion on the top of it. The doctor said it's probably nothing, but with my history and my family history, they don't want to take the chance. I think most of the family is still numb about my sister. It does not seem real that she is gone. My sister Nanette is working on the program for the memorial. After looking at her pictures at different stages of her life it hits you. The memorial is set for Saturday 8/21, 10a.m. at my mother's church. It's so strange listening to arrangements being made for my sister who was dancing 5 months ago. No one knows from day to day what life will bring, so you have to live the life you are given.

Royce from NYU hasn't called me since last week. I will call him so that I can get on with the story for the website about my robotic surgery.

Thursday, August 19, 2010 9:26 AM

Sometimes I have days or hours when I forget that I had cancer, then there are days that I think about it a lot. Because my sister's battle has ended, I think about it a lot. I hear the word more and more. People are calling about flowers and we are telling them to make a donation to a cancer organization of their choice in her name. As it gets closer to her memorial it's becoming real. The pictures, the flowers, the calls, the visitors make it more real.

Saturday, August 21, 2010 7:43 AM

This is the morning of my sister's memorial. Her body was cremated yesterday. Family has been flying in and friends are stopping by. I made the fresh flower arrangements for the luncheon tables, (which was a first for me). I made small arrangements in little inspirational cups. I didn't sleep well and I wish that I didn't have to face today but I do. I want to be there for my mother who lost a daughter, my nephew and niece, who lost a mother and for my children who have a fear of losing their mother. Nine months and 19 days after finding out that I had cancer, I'm honoring my sister who won her battle with breast cancer 7 years ago but lost this round.

Sunday, August 22, 2010 7:43 AM

Over 300 people showed up yesterday to remember my sister. Friends and family, people who never met her and some who knew her all her life. I saw life in motion yesterday. Babies I used to hold, holding their babies now; childhood friends on canes; elderly grandparents being helped by strong grown grandchildren. A lot of tears and laughter (thank GOD). More laughter than tears. A lot of "why do we only get together at times like this". A lot of hugs and holding on to each other. My children standing close to me, telling me to sit down, get a plate, eat some food. Telling me how good I look, asking how I'm feeling, still scared, still looking out for me.

What my sister Irene left me:

Wings to fly, to finish my journal, to not care about what other people think, to live life as an adventure. Peace: to stay in no matter what the moment brings. But most of all she left me the Baton to fight this crazy disease called CANCER.

AMEN

Faith Into Action

The Ministry

I can't remember the date, but it was a Sunday when Beverly Norman Thomas was singing, and her song turned into a testimony about her battle with breast cancer. Our church has about 900 to 1,000 in attendance, but somehow when the doors open after service it was only Beverly and I in the outer hall (I mean that's how I saw it). I told her I was a survivor, we hugged. More people started talking about the battle. People started giving me phone numbers of people in the battle. "Call them, encourage them", was the message. Let them know they are not alone. A few Sundays later Beverly marched me into Rev. Clarence Norman's office in the middle of him having a meeting with Rev. Bloodsaw (assistant Pastor then, now Pastor and Rev. Dr. Bloodsaw). Her words were, "Dad this is the lady I told you about with the cancer ministry". I was in a daze, but I think he said, "Let's get it going".

Tuesday, January 2014

Our first meeting with maybe 6 people - Rev. Christine, Francine (whose daughter had cancer at age 2 and now is a resident at New York University Oncology on her way to becoming a doctor), Sister Virginia Cheese (whose husband was battling prostate cancer, Mildred Scott (a breast cancer survivor of about 15 years), Pat Razor, (another breast cancer survivor of many years) and Bro Charles (a survivor of prostate cancer). It was the fourth Tuesday at 6 p.m. at 450 Eastern Parkway, Brooklyn NY, in the Nursery of the First Baptist Church of Crown Heights that the Cancer Ministry was finally born. "Rosalind, you'll be the President", I was told. My answer, "My awesome GOD is the President and through him I sit in this chair. I'll be the Chairperson". Francine said this was the Ministry she was led to join because every time I mentioned the ministry the spirit urged her to be involved (she is a long time member of First Baptist and this is the only ministry she's in). She became Co-chairperson. Rev. Christine, my teacher, my Sister-in-Christ, my friend and my encourager is the Spiritual Advisor. Oh, by the way, she is also our personal bookstore (smile). Every book she can find about cancer she has blessed the ministry with.

Our Motto

"Our Faith in GOD is GREATER Than Our Fear of Cancer"

First Baptist Church of Crown Heights - first time walking with American Cancer Society - October 2014. Over 100 members, their families and friends, turned out wearing our purple t-shirts with the motto. Rev. Beaulah E. Smith (a survivor), led us in prayer before we started walking. Did you ever see your dream walking? We had members that couldn't make the walk join us in our prayer circle before we started. Brenda Bloodsaw carried the youngest member in her womb. What a day! We raised five thousand dollars that day. Most of all we strengthened our faith and witnessed our healing.

Saturday April 25, 2015 was the date of our first Cancer Awareness day at First Baptist. Small group discussions were led by survivors of different cancers. We even had a table that you could talk to caregivers. We had speakers from SHARE and Gilda's Club that gave much needed information.

"The battle is not yours, it is the LORD's"

During the last three and a half years of the Cancer Ministry we have lost five active members (one died of complications not related to Cancer). Each one left not only an empty seat at the table but a smile on our faces, a place in our hearts, a tear in our eyes, stronger faith and a will to fight on with dignity. I have visited homes, hospitals and hospice and left lifted by the faith of people in the battle. I have learned that sometimes healing is on the other side.

In February 2013 I lost my cancer buddy Pat Henry. No matter what the doctors told her, she fought on. I have seen people take new drugs - new methods that stopped the growth for a while. I have seen people battle one cancer, have it cured and then have it turn up three more places and still battle on. I have said GOD must be using me because I'm still here. Over the years I have had a few scares but Thank GOD all were negative. There is a certain facial expression you can see when they talk about this intruder in their bodies. It's like the nerve of this tumor trying to find a permanent home in their bodies. It's becomes a physical, mental and spiritual fight at the same time.

It amazes me that so many people fight this battle alone. Family, friends, and co-workers sometimes shy away (like the person is a modern-day leper). I feel sometimes they just don't know what to do or say. I always tell them, "Just listen" or tell them they can say "Tell me what you need from me".

The ministry is a blessing to others.

One of our original members (and most times the only man at the meetings), said that he was embarrassed and depressed about his cancer until he found the cancer ministry. That was one of the smallest but greatest moments for me at the same time. At the meetings, we lift each other up. Conversation can go from what we are feeling, to medical breakthrough, to other people we know that are fighting, to people who don't want treatment, people who are angry about their diagnosis etc. There are hardly any tears, always laughter. One young man in our group (who we assumed was bald), wanted to know when his hair was going to grow back. I can't tell you how many times someone has called or approached me to ask if they could give my phone number to someone. The answer is always yes, that's what I'm here for. I always wear a survivor button when I am out and about.

I work at Brooklyn and New York Cruise Terminals (part time in the Fall mostly). I have so many stories about people and conversations that I have had (it could be a book by itself)! Two that stand out the most both happened at the Brooklyn Pier.

In 2016 the line to check-in was empty and a man was about 20 feet away. I heard a direction agent direct him to a check-in agent. The man said, "I want to go to Rosalind", I know that he couldn't read my name tag from that far away, in fact I didn't even have it on. When he got to the counter he said "Hello, Rosalind". I guessed by the way I looked he realized that I was puzzled because he said, "You don't remember me". He said, "I passed through here last year this time. While you checked me in, I told you that I was battling cancer and the doctors didn't give me much hope. You talked to me awhile and told me that doctors don't have the final say and that you will pray for me". He said, "I'm back and want to tell you that I'm in remission".

In 2017, getting ready to close my computer to go home, I saw a lady, by herself, waiting to check in. Something said, "Check her in". After noticing my button, she asked me what I was a survivor of. I told her, "Uterine cancer - seven and a half years". She told me she was traveling alone because her husband of forty-four years died from lung cancer and that they had planned this trip together for years. She said that he started feeling tired, they went to the doctor, they gave him a PET scan. He had lung cancer and within four weeks he was gone. I left the desk and went around the counter and we hugged each other with tears in our eyes. She told me that she needed me this day and at this time. I told her that GOD was intentional because before I looked up and saw her, I was on my way home.

One of our faithful members is Sister Virginia Cheese, a warm and loving sister-in-Christ. She was a caregiver for her husband and partner for over fifty years, while he battled for years. (Did she take care of him for 50 years???) Even after her husband's death, she is at every meeting if she is in town. I went to an event and they had all kinds of buttons for cancer. I picked up a simple button that said Caregiver and gave it to Sister Virginia about three years ago. I met her daughter on our very first cancer walk in 2014, when she found out that I was the person who gave her Mother the button she said I have to give you a hug "My Mother loves that button". Virginia is still wearing that button years after her husband's passing.

June 2017, National Cancer Survivors Month

Rev. Bloodsaw said a special prayer for the Cancer Ministry. Before service was over, he asked that survivors stand up. Then he said, "Look at them. If they survived, you can too!" That day I met a woman who had survived forty-four years since her Breast Cancer diagnosis.

Thursday, June 27, 2017

I have been wondering why I can't seem to finish this journal (editing problems etc.) I now know why.

Fast forward. It's 7 years later - 2017

Where do I start?

I kept wondering "What is my purpose"? Why was I the only one that I started this cancer battle with that is still alive? Women in the group with me at Gilda's club are all gone. The last one was my cancer buddy and friend, Pat Henry. People that I meet on this journey from 2009 to 2013 are all gone. My son Craig once asked me do I have feelings of guilt. "No" was my answer, "Only feelings of being blessed". God wants to use me, but I don't know how. "What about a blog", I was asked? "No. I'm not a computer person", was my answer. Service? "Yes, but what kind?" I believe in customer services. My prayer became "Lord, please order my steps".

Way before cancer, I kept saying GOD was trying to tell me something. Now I have time to slow down and listen. Get a group together to comfort, tell their stories and encourage each other. Ask can we have meetings in the Church. I started going to Women's Bible Study bi-monthly with a great bunch of women that I felt comfortable with (women of purpose, faith and who were trying to grow on this walk). Our teacher was and still is Rev. Christine Caton (now Rev. Dr. Christine). I can't tell you when or what made me start telling the ladies about what GOD had placed on my heart. No one ever tried to discourage me, they listened and smiled. For about two and a half years I talked about it. One day during that time Rev. Christine told me it would have to be a ministry. I explained/questioned how that could be. I'm not a Minister. Her answer was any group that starts in the church is considered a ministry if it ministers to people. "Back down Rosalind. You are not qualified", was the voice in my head. But with prayer and determination I asked God to order my steps. More and more people in the church were sharing they had cancer, a loved one was in the battle or that someone just lost the battle. I kept on talking about wanting to start the ministry. Poor Rev. Christine, I would not let up with her. She jokes now that I kept piercing her in the side. Then one bright Sunday morning, during an usher's meeting, Rev. Christine found me and told me that things might be looking better to get the ministry going. I cried so much that one of the ushers asked me "what did she say to you"?

"Wait on the Lord and be of good courage"

Sunday, July 30, 2017

The International Ministry of First Baptist has their 2nd Annual International Worship Service. Special guest: First Baptist Cancer Ministry. What an honor. The guest Preacher was Rev. Garvey C. Ince. He gave a wonderful message of faith, hope and not giving up. After he finished and sat down, he waited 10 minutes and got back up and said that he was led to give a testimony because he believed that someone needed to hear it. He told a story about being laid off 13 years ago. Six months later he was told that he had lung cancer. He said that he had made his peace with God and told his family that he was okay with it. He said that on his last day of Chemotherapy someone came into the treatment room and said, "I don't know who I'm talking to, but GOD said don't give up".

The Cancer Ministry received a card with lovely words and a donation from the International Ministry. That day was real emotional day for me and looking at this Journal and where GOD is leading me is almost unbelievable, but I know that God is ordering my steps because I wouldn't have chosen or imagine this Journey on my own. My faith comforts me. I have found peace and joy in so many ways walking this path. I have been encouraged, blessed and comforted and I'm only trying to give this back to others while they or a loved one battles.

Saturday, September 23, 2017

The Cancer Ministry hosted a Cancer Ministry Awareness Day. It was well attended with speakers from NYU Langone Cancer Center, TEAL, SHARE, Gilda's Club, and a few Survivors that told their stories about their journey with cancer. It was an outreach for the community at large with information and giveaways. I have been asked to speak about my journey at luncheons, on panels, at schools and various other functions. For 3 years I have walked at Delta airlines Relay-for-Life, and participated in many fundraisers. I've even been interviewed by a local filmmaker and my story runs on a local cable network here in New York City.

I've met so many souls along this journey, cried so many tears of joy and sorrow and laughed until I've cried. I have held on through so many storms and been held up by so many strong arms.

Thank God, I'm still on the battlefield.

Rosalind Pettiford
Author, Survivor

A Prayer for This Season

Lord,

You've allowed this difficult season in my life. Remind me in my times of struggle, sadness, and frustration that this, indeed, is a season. It will have its end. Let this season not consume me or deceive my spirit into hopelessness, but instead sharpen and teach me; strengthen and use me for your glory. Speak to my heart, encourage me, lord. Walk with me.

You've allowed this difficult season in my life. Remind me in my times of struggle, sadness, and frustration that this, indeed, is a season. It will have its end. Let this season not consume me or deceive my spirit into hopelessness, but instead sharpen and teach me; strengthen and use me for your glory. Speak to my heart, encourage me, lord. Walk with me.

Amen